Little People, **BIG DREAMS**™

SALVADOR DALÍ

Written by
Maria Isabel Sánchez Vegara

Illustrated by
Mariona Tolosa Sisteré

Frances Lincoln
Children's Books

In the small town of Figueres, Spain, there lived a rich family who had an eccentric child named Salvador. He got his name from an older brother who sadly passed away nine months before Salvador was born.

SALVADOR
DALÍ
OCTOBER 12, 1901
AUGUST 1, 1903

His parents rarely said no to any of his wishes,
no matter how unusual they were. So Salvador let his
imagination run wild. He believed he was destined for
an extraordinary life, and he was determined to live it.

Yet, school was a different story for Salvador.
The other children used to laugh at his peculiar ways.

The only thing he looked forward to was summer,
when the family visited Cadaqués, a fishing village
where he would draw under the sun.

At home, Salvador used a small laundry room on the roof as an art studio. There, he spent hours painting and studying the work of great artists. He was sure that one day he would be remembered as one of them.

He was just fourteen when his art appeared in a local exhibition. It was such a success that, three years later, his family decided to send him to study at the Royal Academy of Fine Arts in Madrid, the best painting school in Spain.

In Madrid, however, Salvador spent his mornings
bored to tears by his old-fashioned teachers.

Fortunately, his evenings were filled with long conversations about the new art trends in Paris. One in particular caught his attention: it was called Surrealism.

The Surrealists were a group started by a French writer named André Breton. They were not interested in the real world, but in bringing their dreams to life through art. Salvador would do anything to be part of their crew!

His chance came sooner than expected when his friend Luis Buñuel asked for his help to make a film. It was full of images that didn't make sense, which is why the Surrealists loved it! Salvador was soon welcomed into the club.

It was during a summer in Cadaqués with some fellow artists that he met his lifelong partner, Gala. A tiny fishing hut became their hideout, and Salvador left his mark by hanging one of his teeth from the ceiling.

He was one of Europe's best-known Surrealist artists when, one day, an idea came to him after eating some gooey cheese: to paint melting clocks. The picture became a sensation and gave him his big break in New York City.

Soon his work was all over the city. He designed furniture and hats, wrote books, painted theater sets, and created shop-window displays. The Americans were so taken with him that Gala and Salvador moved there for years.

MOMA

THE SECRET
LIFE of
SALVADOR DALÍ

Dear Salvado...

Back in Spain, Salvador turned from Surrealism to more
traditional painting, but he never stopped seeking attention.
Later, he focused on setting up a museum dedicated
to himself. After all, his own life was his greatest work of art.

And little Salvador kept waking up every morning asking himself the same question: What wonderful things will I achieve today? This is a question worth asking ourselves if we want to live each day to the fullest.

SALVADOR DALÍ

(Born 1904 – Died 1989)

1929   1939

Salvador Dalí was born in the Catalonian town of Figueres in northeast
Spain. He grew up an eccentric, dreamy child, with an incredible gift
for art. At age seventeen, he was admitted to the prestigious San Fernando
Royal Academy of Fine Arts in Madrid—only to be expelled four years later
when he refused to take tests given by his professors, claiming that he was
more intelligent than them! Back home, his reputation as an artist began
to grow and, in 1929, he moved to Paris, home to the group known as the
Surrealists, who were interested in exploring the unconscious mind. With his
friend Luis Buñuel, Salvador made a film called *Un Chien Andalou*, which
became a Surrealist sensation. That year, he met his future wife, Gala and,
not long after, his art began to receive wider attention. His 1931 painting

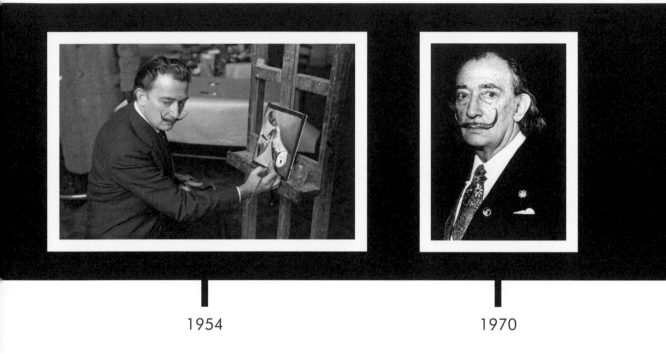

1954

1970

The Persistence of Memory, featuring melting watches in a dreamlike landscape, helped him become the world's best-known Surrealist artist. By 1936, he was on the cover of *Time* magazine. It wasn't just Salvador's art that made him famous, but his attention-seeking stunts—he arrived at one exhibition wearing a deep-sea diving suit! When the Second World War broke out, Salvador and Gala moved to the USA, returning to Spain in 1948. Salvador continued to create excitement wherever he went and even showed up at one event in a car stuffed with cauliflowers! When he was seventy, he opened the Dalí Theatre-Museum in Figueres, a museum full of his brilliant and bizarre artwork. Salvador's story shows us that great things can happen when we believe in ourselves and dare to be different.

Want to find out more about **Salvador Dalí**?

Have a read of this great book:

Who Was Salvador Dalí? by Paula K. Manzanero and Gregory Copeland

If you're in Figueres, Spain, you can visit the Dalí Theatre-Museum.

Text © 2024 Maria Isabel Sánchez Vegara. Illustrations © 2024 Mariona Tolosa Sisteré
Original idea of the series by Maria Isabel Sánchez Vegara, published by Alba Editorial, s.l.u.
"Little People, BIG DREAMS" and "Pequeña & Grande" are trademarks of
Alba Editorial s.l.u. and/or Beautifool Couple S.L.
First published in the US in 2024 by Frances Lincoln Children's Books, an imprint of The Quarto Group.
Quarto Boston North Shore, 100 Cummings Center, Suite 265D, Beverly, MA 01915, USA
Tel: +1 978-282-9590 **www.Quarto.com**
All rights reserved.
No part of this publication may be reproduced, stored in a retrieval system, or transmitted, in any form,
or by any means, electrical, mechanical, photocopying, recording or otherwise without the prior written
permission of the publisher or a license permitting restricted copying.

This book is not authorized, licensed, or approved by the estate of Salvador Dalí.
Any faults are the publisher's who will be happy to rectify for future printings.
A CIP record for this book is available from the Library of Congress.
ISBN 978-1-83600-020-4
Set in Futura BT.

Published by Peter Marley · Designed by Sasha Moxon
Commissioned by Lucy Menzies · Edited by Claire Saunders
Editorial Assistance from Molly Mead · Production by Robin Boothroyd
Manufactured in Guangdong, China CC072024
1 3 5 7 9 8 6 4 2

Photographic acknowledgments (pages 28-29, from left to right): 1. Portrait of Salvador Dali 1929 France © Photo 12/Archives Snark
via Alamy Stock Photo. 2. SALVADOR DALI (1904-1989). Spanish painter. Photograph by Carl Van Vechten, 29 November 1939 ©
GRANGER - Historical Picture Archive / Granger, NYC via Alamy Stock Photo. 3. Salvador Dali at the Musée du Louvre Paris 1954
© Photo 12 / Photo12.com, Descharnes, via Alamy Stock Photo. 4. Portrait of artist Salvador Dali © Keystone Press / KEYSTONE
Pictures USA via Alamy Stock Photo.

MIX
Paper | Supporting
responsible forestry
FSC® C008047
FSC
www.fsc.org

Collect the Little People, BIG DREAMS™ series:

| FRIDA KAHLO | COCO CHANEL | MAYA ANGELOU | AMELIA EARHART | AGATHA CHRISTIE | MARIE CURIE | ROSA PARKS | AUDREY HEPBURN | EMMELINE PANKHURST |

| ELLA FITZGERALD | ADA LOVELACE | JANE AUSTEN | GEORGIA O'KEEFFE | HARRIET TUBMAN | ANNE FRANK | MOTHER TERESA | JOSEPHINE BAKER | L. M. MONTGOMERY |

| JANE GOODALL | SIMONE DE BEAUVOIR | MUHAMMAD ALI | STEPHEN HAWKING | MARIA MONTESSORI | VIVIENNE WESTWOOD | MAHATMA GANDHI | DAVID BOWIE | WILMA RUDOLPH |

| DOLLY PARTON | BRUCE LEE | RUDOLF NUREYEV | ZAHA HADID | MARY SHELLEY | MARTIN LUTHER KING JR. | DAVID ATTENBOROUGH | ASTRID LINDGREN | EVONNE GOOLAGONG |

| BOB DYLAN | ALAN TURING | BILLIE JEAN KING | GRETA THUNBERG | JESSE OWENS | JEAN-MICHEL BASQUIAT | ARETHA FRANKLIN | CORAZON AQUINO | PELÉ |

| ERNEST SHACKLETON | STEVE JOBS | AYRTON SENNA | LOUISE BOURGEOIS | ELTON JOHN | JOHN LENNON | PRINCE | CHARLES DARWIN | CAPTAIN TOM MOORE |

| HANS CHRISTIAN ANDERSEN | STEVIE WONDER | MEGAN RAPINOE | MARY ANNING | MALALA YOUSAFZAI | ANDY WARHOL | RUPAUL | MICHELLE OBAMA | MINDY KALING |

| IRIS APFEL | ROSALIND FRANKLIN | RUTH BADER GINSBURG | MARILYN MONROE | KAMALA HARRIS | ALBERT EINSTEIN | CHARLES DICKENS | YOKO ONO | MICHAEL JORDAN |

NELSON MANDELA	PABLO PICASSO	AMANDA GORMAN	GLORIA STEINEM	FLORENCE NIGHTINGALE	HARRY HOUDINI	J.R.R. TOLKIEN	ELVIS PRESLEY	NEIL ARMSTRONG
ALEXANDER VON HUMBOLDT	NIKOLA TESLA	WILMA MANKILLER	MARCUS RASHFORD	LAVERNE COX	MAE JEMISON	DWAYNE JOHNSON	HELEN KELLER	ANNA PAVLOVA
QUEEN ELIZABETH	TERRY FOX	HEDY LAMARR	SHAKIRA	FREDDIE MERCURY	LEWIS HAMILTON	LOUIS PASTEUR	PRINCESS DIANA	DAVID HOCKNEY
VANESSA NAKATE	OLIVE MORRIS	KING CHARLES	MOZART	STEVE IRWIN	JÜRGEN KLOPP	LEO MESSI	SALLY RIDE	TENZING NORGAY
KYLIE MINOGUE	BEYONCÉ	TAYLOR SWIFT	RAFA NADAL	USAIN BOLT	SIMONE BILES	STAN LEE	LEONARD COHEN	DAVID BECKHAM

VINCENT VAN GOGH
MARY KOM
SALVADOR DALÍ

Scan the QR code for free activity sheets, teachers' notes and more information about the series at www.littlepeoplebigdreams.com